THE ILLUSTRATED HISTORY OF
MOTORCYCLES

THE ILLUSTRATED
HISTORY OF
MOTORCYCLES

Erwin Tragatsch

Quantum
Books

A QUANTUM BOOK

This book is produced by
Quantum Publishing Ltd.
6 Blundell Street
London N7 9BH

This edition printed 2003

ISBN 1-86160-679-6

QUMIHOM

Phototypeset in England by Filmtype Services Limited,
Scarborough
Colour Separation by Sakai Lithocolour Company
Limited, Hong Kong
Printed in Singapore by
Star Standard Industries Pte Ltd.

CONTENTS

INTRODUCTION

The author, on a 498cc four-cylinder Gilera works racing machine.

THIS ENCYCLOPEDIA lists in alphabetical sequence more than 2,500 makes of motorcycle, produced in at least 30 countries, from 1894 to the present day. The companies' commercial and sporting histories and their ranges of models, whether great or small, are discussed. Facts, figures, dates and technical details are provided. Many of the entries are illustrated, sometimes with hitherto-unpublished photographs.

Some of the early firms listed were very small, and assembled their machines entirely from bought-in parts, but all of them made production motorcycles. Companies which produced only 'one-offs', or which were merely workshops or dealers, are not included. The principal engines used by each manufacturer are detailed, and there are additional lists of important proprietary engines. There are also separate lists showing the major models of motorcycle produced throughout the world during interesting periods in the history of the industry.

I believe this to be the most comprehensive book of its kind, and I hope that it will be interesting not only to the motorcycle technician, dealer and sportsman but also to the collector, owner (past or present) or simply the enthusiast. When I began to compile my previous book *The World's Motorcycles, 1894–1963,* some of my friends in the industry suggested that I had engaged myself in an impossible task. When the book was published, it became a best-seller, filling a gap in the bookshelves of many a motorcycle enthusiast. That success led to the compilation of a much bigger book, with its extensive illustration. This latest edition has been completely updated, new photographs have been included and some existing ones superseded by better illustrations.

My involvement with motorcycles has been lifelong. I have worked within the industry itself, in the motorcycle trade, in motor-sport, and in the motoring Press. My own experience, and widespread international research over a long period, have helped me fill the pages which follow. I have been helped by veteran riders, designers, manufacturers and their employees, many of them personal friends. Some of them have provided from memory details of machines which were built many decades ago.

Acquaintanceships have been renewed, and pleasant times recalled. It may have been 'impossible', but it was thoroughly enjoyable. I hope you enjoy it, too.

Erwin Tragatsch

THE PIONEER YEARS

In the second half of the 19th century, both in Europe and in the USA, there were a good many attempts to build a practical steam bicycle. None was truly successful. Reducing engine and steam system to a manageable size and weight almost inevitably compromised power output and reliability, but the real drawback was the speed with which any steam engine evaporated its water. Topping-up the boiler feed water tank every ten or 15 miles was hardly convenient, or indeed always possible, while carrying a reserve supply was no answer at all. Few people did more to further the cause of the light steam-powered vehicle than the famous Count de Dion, yet his first sight of a very early petrol-engined car was enough to convince him that here lay the future. For all his success hitherto with steam, it was to the internal combustion engine that he immediately turned.

The internal combustion engine itself went through a considerable period of development and refinement. The earliest gas engines had no compression stroke and so were extremely inefficient. Etienne Lenoir's commercially successful workshop engine of 1860 drew in gas and air for half of one stroke, whereupon it was ignited, the subsequent expansion providing what power there was. Exhaust took place on the return stroke. The engine was 'double acting' — ignition took place on both sides of the piston. The four-stroke cycle of induction, compression, expansion and exhaust, proposed by French railway engineer Alphonse Beau de Rochas in 1862, was first attempted — and patented — by Nikolaus Otto of the Deutz gas engine works in Germany in 1876. Nine years later,

Otto's one-time colleagues, Gottlieb Daimler and Paul Maybach, tested a liquid-fuelled four stroke engine in a two wheeled chassis they called the 'Einspur'. Often spoken of as the world's first motorcycle, the Einspur, of course, was intended to test only the engine, but, in fact, it was a remarkably well thought-out and practical vehicle for its time.

Daimler's engine was astonishingly well adapted to automotive use. Light and self-contained, it was of 270cc, with the flywheel assembly enclosed in a cast aluminium crankcase, with a fan-cooled cast iron cylinder and cylinder head. The inlet valve opened automatically, while the exhaust valve was pushrod operated from a camtrack in the face of one of the flywheels. The 'benzene' (petrol) fuel was vaporised by passing air over its surface in a carburettor. Mistrusting electrical ignition, the inventors used a 'hot tube' of platinum, heated externally by a petrol-fuelled burner. The engine ran at the then remarkable speed of 800rpm, and produced something like half a horsepower.

That Europe was indeed ready for the automotive engine in 1885 is shown by the almost simultaneous appearance of petrol engined tricars from Karl Benz in Germany and Edward Butler in England. Of the two, Butler's was in its later, developed form far the more sophisticated, but repressive British traffic laws, not repealed until 1896, prevented it ever reaching commercial production. Butler's engine was fitted with rotary valves, a sort of primitive 'magneto' (actually dependent on the generation of static electricity rather than magnetic flux) and a spray carburettor, rather than a surface vaporiser.

Butler's patent on the carburettor prevented later inventors from obtaining a monopoly.

Count Albert De Dion and his partner Georges Bouton of the firm of De Dion, Bouton, probably did as much — and more — than anyone else to further the cause of the early motorcycle. They themselves concentrated in the 1890s on petrol-engined tricycles rather than on two wheelers, but their single-cylinder engine was suitable for both. In 1897 De Dion, Bouton offered these engines for sale to all comers, thus enabling scores of experimenters to copy — and improve upon — the remarkably successful machine popularised by the Werner brothers. As a result, the De Dion engine was copied — with and without acknowledgement — and made under licence all over the world, In its early form, the De Dion was of 70mm × 70mm 270cc, which was very soon uprated to 86mm × 86mm 500cc. As an indication of the De Dion's outstanding penetration of the market, it was significant that these were the engine dimensions chosen by Britain's newly formed Auto Cycle Club in 1903, when it came to standardise capacity classes for competition.

The engine was entirely conventional with air cooling, automatic inlet valve, surface carburettor and battery and coil ignition. However, it set new standards in precision engineering and provided a bench mark for power and reliability by which all other contemporary engines were judged. Needless to say, it soon had many rivals, of which the Belgian Minerva and the French Clement were the most popular, while inventors were quick to improve on the basic concept. As early as

Germany's Hildebrand and Wolfmuller Motorrad (left, top), the world's first production motor cycle. By the 1920s, BMW was leading the German industry, with its methodical production approach (left, bottom).

Infinitely variable ratio belt drive as used by Rudge (left, bottom). The pulleys expanded and contracted in sympathy to keep the belt adjusted. The 550cc side-valve Triumph, in the three-speed Sturmey Archer countershaft gearbox, was introduced in 1915 (right, bottom).

1898 in Britain, Coventry's Percy Riley, later to become a famous car maker, built an engine with a mechanically operated inlet valve, and went on to develop (and patent) 'overlap' valve timing. There were spray carburettors in profusion, one of the best of which was the British Amac of 1903. The hated and unreliable battery and coil ignition system was gradually superseded by the magneto, perfected through the work of Frederick Simms in England and Robert Bosch in Stuttgart in collaboration, first as a low-tension system and, then in 1902 as a high-tension one with rotating armature. (As a result of Bosch's developments, high tension magnetos became a virtual German monopoly, which led to some practical difficulties on the outbreak of the First World War in 1914).

Early development of the motorcycle seemed best advanced when it was left to the instincts of 'practical men' — gifted amateurs and superior blacksmiths, rather than formal engineers. This is no doubt a gross oversimplification, but certainly the purpose-designed Hildebrand and Wolfmuller Motorrad of 1894 was a failure, as was the equally impressive four-cylinder motor cycle designed by Colonel Holden — later to design the Brooklands track — a few years later. Both employed direct drive via the exposed connecting rods to crank axles on the rear spindle, which naturally severely limited engine speed and flywheel effect. In point of fact, the Motorrad had a capacity of no less than 1490cc, and made about 2hp at 380 rpm — at which engine speed of about 25mph was attained. All that bulk, weight and complication produced a performance that was put to shame by the Werner brothers' crude Motocyclette.

From time to time, other engineers took a look at the motorcycle of their day and decided that they could do better. In 1908, for instance T W Badgery of the James Cycle Co commissioned a design from the well thought of consulting engineer P L Renouf, which was the sensation of that year's London Motor Cycle Show. The 'Safety James' had a tubular chassis on car lines, centre-hub steering, quickly detachable wheels on single sided stub axles, and internal expanding brakes fore and aft. It had a 500cc single cylinder SV engine of James' own make, and belt drive, with an engine-pulley clutch. Alas, it was a monumental flop, and the James company rapidly turned to more orthodox designs. The response to the four-cylinder air-cooled 680cc Wilkinson TAC and later 850cc water-cooled TMC models was also disappointing. For 1910 and 1912, these offered truly advanced and luxurious specifications, but failed to sell in realistic numbers.

It seemed as though motor cycle design had to advance a bit at a time, not too precipitately and never too boldly. To be sure, Alfred Scott's radical two stroke twin of 1909 (1908 if you count six prototypes built by Jowett Brothers for development) found a market — but never a large one, even after Scott's TT wins in 1912 and 1913. And, in retrospect, the wonder is that the Scott sold at all, for not only was the two-stroke engine virtually unheard of, but this one was a twin and was partly — very soon fully — watercooled. The straight-tube triangulated frame, and the cylindrical fuel tank embracing the saddle tube must also have looked very strange to the average motor cyclist of 1909.

One of the Scott's most striking features was that it had a kickstarter — the first ever offered — and so the engine could be started at rest, and the machine moved off by engaging the lower of two 'gears' — actually two separate primary chains driving two sprockets on a countershaft with expanding clutches. The kickstart apart, there was nothing new about this. P & M, for one, had long since offered such a gear, as had many of the large V twin 'tricars' that were popular between about 1904 and 1909. What riders were demanding at about the same time as the Scott made its appearance, was a 'free engine' or clutch, and it was a big selling point for Triumph when they fitted a multi-plate clutch in the rear hub in 1909. There were, of course, even then, numerous proprietary clutches, usually incorporated in a special belt pulley.

Sprung front forks started to become really popular in about 1907. Again, many were proprietary fittings designed for use on older machines, though, for example, Quadrant had had such a front fork since 1903, while Rex had fitted them as standard since 1906.

Some of the early designs look downright dangerous to modern eyes, and probably were! Once again, the Scott of 1909 had perhaps the best design of all, with a true telescopic action. The famous Druid front fork, with parallel lever action controlled by coil springs first appeared in 1906, and became very popular — almost standard wear on British bikes and in successively modified form — setting a fashion that was to last for 30 odd years and more.

Spring frames were the subject of many an invention in the early years, though very few of them had much merit. Curiously, those that enjoyed a certain success, such as the BAT, the Zenette and the much later Edmund, were not really spring frames at all, but sprung sub-frames, whereby the saddle and footrests were isolated together from road shocks. Such systems did absolutely nothing to help to

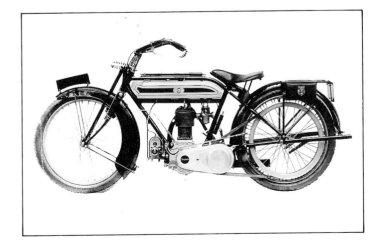

keep the rear wheel in contact with the road.

Lighting remained an afterthought. Few people rode at night in any case, and very few motor cycles were sold with lights of any sort. At first, cycle oil lamps were used, and sturdier versions were soon made. But from an early date, acetylene gas lighting became available and was soon accepted as standard. It might be messy and demand considerable looking after, but it was comparatively reliable and cheap.

As for brakes, the less said the better! Even so meticulous an engineer as Alfred Scott could at that time see no further than a cycle type stirrup at the front, and a shoe bearing on the inside of a drum formed in the rear chain sprocket. Front brakes were in any case regarded as mere 'bobby dodgers' not to be used — in the first place because they damaged the paint and plating of the front rim, but also because of the firm conviction that front brakes were dangerous. This superstition was a long time a-dying. As late as the 1960s a national survey in Britain found that over 40% of motor cyclists never used the front brake!

Change speed gears were a fruitful field for inventors in those early years. The 'adjustable pulley' was an early development, usually sold as a proprietary item and a not terribly satisfactory one at that. Early competition riders would carry two belts — one for use on the level, with the pulley flanges screwed close together to give a high ratio. When a freak hill had to be climbed, the pulley flanges were screwed apart and a slightly shorter belt fitted. The once famous Zenith Gradua and Rudge Multi systems were extensions of this idea. These took mechanical control of the driving pulley and, in the case of Zenith, actually automatically extended, or shortened, the wheelbase of the motor cycle to keep the belt taut. The Rudge Multi's rear pully flanges moved in and out in reverse sympathy with those on the engine pulley.

Quite a few simple two speed epicyclic gears — notably the NSU — made an early appearance, and eventually migrated to the rear hub in bicycle fashion. Such three-speed Armstong hubs featured strongly in the results of the 1911 Junior TT, held for the first time on the Mountain circuit in the Isle of

Early days in France and Germany. Above left: The first Daimler and Maybach two-wheeler. Left: The De Dion-Bouton three-wheeler. Above: Road conditions contrasted infavourably with those of the track. Right: Tessler tweaks a speed record on a British BAT in 1903.

THOSE MAGNIFICENT MEN ON THEIR CYCLING MACHINES

A steam engine, fired by petrol, powered this von Sauerbronn-Davis velocipede, 1883

The 1887 Millet prototype had a radial engine similar to those later used in aircraft

Propellor power . . . a chitty, chitty, bang bike by Anzani had its test flight in 1906

Look, no pedals! An ordinary bicycle gets a shove from an auxiliary engine . . . Italy, 1893

'Luxurious, high-powered, all-weather car-ette' . . . twin engined Quadrant, made in Britain, 1905

Where to put the engine? Above the front wheel, perhaps? That (1) was Werner's solution, in 1899. Enfield placed the engine in the same place, but to drive the rear wheel

Strange layouts abounded at the turn of the century . . . Singer positioned the engine in the hub of the front wheel (2). Further variations came from British Excelsior (3), Phelon and Moore (4), Hildebrand and Wolfmüller (5), Beeston (6), Ormonde (7), Singer again (8) and Humber (9).

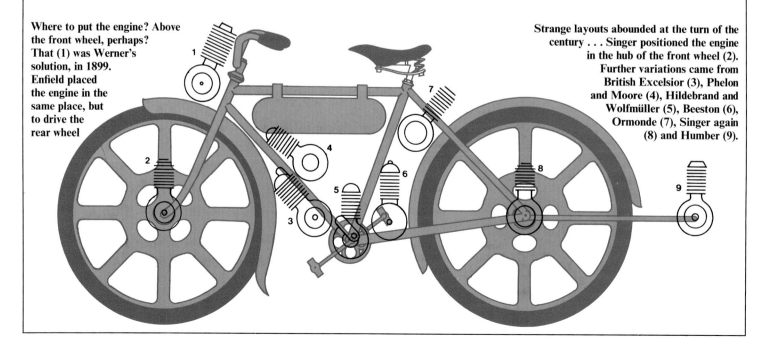

In Czechoslovakia, Laurin & Klement produced the elegant single-cylinder B–D in 1903 (top), and more sporting versions such as the V-twin CCR (below). Bottom: Ludwig Opel with a 2¾ hp Opel motorcycle on army manoeuvres in 1905.

An early Scott two-stroke with water-cooled cylinder heads and air-cooled cylinders, telescopic front forks and all-chain drive (below) Acetylene powered this early headlamp (bottom).

Man. But the Indians that finished 1-2-3 in the Senior race that year, used countershaft gear-boxes, and these made a big impression. Development of such gearboxes was rapid, and their wide acceptance really dated from the use by the Triumph company of the superb Sturmey Archer gearbox and clutch in their late Veteran masterpiece, the 550cc model H of despatch rider fame in the war years between 1914 and 1918.

Throughout the era, the side-valve engine reigned supreme. The ohv layout occasionally appeared for racing, but showed no great superiority. The theoretical advantages of overhead valves were, with compression ratios of about 4-1, more apparent than real, and valve steels being what they then were, the ohv layout was widely mistrusted for its threat of mechanical carnage from a 'dropped' valve. Pistons were universally of cast iron, though racing pistons were painstakingly (and expensively) machined from steel.

Ball and roller bearings were coming into use, especially for racing, but phosphor bronze bushes were still widely used, almost always lubricated by 'spit and hope' total loss systems. These depended upon a simple hand-operated pump transferring oil into the crankcase, whence it was distributed by 'splash'.

Two major companies — JAP, founded in 1903 and Precision dominated the engine scene, as far as Britain was concerned. Though the latter did not start making engines until 1910, their wares rapidly gained a fine reputation. The Stevens brothers of Wolver-hampton had made engines of various sizes before settling for making the 350cc AJS motor cycle, while Dalton & Wade, Blumfeld and half a dozen others, long forgotten, also competed for a place. Of imported engines, the MAG, made by Motosacoche of Geneva, was by far and away the most successful.

Nor were these engines the 'longstrokes' beloved of ill-informed myth, but were mostly near-square in their bore and stroke configur-ation. Towards the end of the period, small capacity V twins became popular, and did well in competitions.

The 'Lightweight' — 250cc — class was hardly established before 1914. By that year, the weak and feeble machines, virtually moto-rised bicycles, that had struggled for a foo-thold in 1900, had become sturdy, powerful and reliable motorcycles that had, in the words of a contemporary writer, 'attained a state very close to perfection'. Such complac-ency invites mockery, but there is no doubt

that, looking back a mere 14 or 15 years, there was some excuse for it. The motor cycle, indeed, had come a long, long way. Few people realised how much further it still had to travel on the road to 'perfection'.

The notorious Devil's Elbow on the T.T. circuit
(main picture) and the start of the first-ever T.T.
race in 1908 (inset) with its winner, Harry
Reed, on his D.O.T. (inset). An Indian came
second the following year, having led for half the
race.

THE AMERICAN STORY

A STEAM-POWERED bicycle built by Sylvanus Roper in 1870 is still preserved in the Smithsonian Museum in Washington DC, the real involvement of the USA in the story of the motorcycle dates from the importation of a De Dion tricycle in 1898 by Hiram Maxim who, at the time, was — among his many other activities — consulting engineer to Colonel A A Pope's Columbia bicycle manufacturing concern. Columbia, in fact, were the first company to offer a motorcycle for sale in the country in 1900; within months, they had a dozen competitors, none of whom offered much more than the crudest of specifications.

In early 1901, however, the Indian, designed by Springfield bicycle maker, George M Hendee, and toolmaker Oscar Hedstrom, made its first appearance. Its strengthened bicycle frame, retaining the pedalling gear, incorporated the single cylinder engine as part of the seat tube, and thus inclined rearwards. It had an automatic inlet valve and an ingenious spray carburettor of Hedstrom's own design, but the engine itself, though designed by Hedstrom was made by the Thor Manufacturing Co, as were all Indian engines until 1905.

From the start, Indian used chain drive to the rear wheel as did most of their rivals. Curiously, one of the few makes to use belt drive — and to persist with it until 1912 — was the Harley Davidson, first produced for sale in 1904. Though Indian sales were modest at first — 143 machines in 1902 — success came quickly, after good showings in early endurance events, and Hendee and Hedstrom

pursued a policy of innovation and improvement. In 1907, when sales were in the thousands, a V twin engine of 600cc was introduced, built by Indian themselves, with the 'Hedstrom motor' cast into the crankcase. One such machine, with twistgrip throttle control and a sprung front fork, was shipped to Britain, where it took part in the ACC's 1000-mile trial, winning a gold medal. Indian were already extremely alive to the possibilities of export to Europe, and especially to Britain.

In 1909, expatriate American W H Wells was made British concessionaire, and entered himself and George Lee Evans in the Senior TT in the Isle of Man. Sensationally, Evans led the race for half its distance, finishing a close second to Matchless rider Harry Collier. In 1910, Indian introduced a two-speed countershaft gearbox and clutch. Already successful at home in pure speed events on board tracks, they now provided Wells' English agency with racing machines that competed with spectacular success at Brooklands. And for the 1911 Senior TT, run for the first time on the famous Mountain circuit, Indian visited in force, with George Hendee himself, Oscar Hedstrom, ace rider Jake de Rosier, and a full compliment of machinery and race mechanics. They meant to win — and win they did, with their British riders taking the first three places. In 1912, Indian's sales reached 20,000.

Not that Indian had it entirely their own way in America in the first decade of the new century. In racing, and especially in board track

arley Davidson favoured belt drive (bottom right), but
w of their competitors followed.

One of the all-conquering Indians in the **1911
Senior T.T.**, seen here at Union Mills. The
rider, **C.B. Franklyn**, was later a leading
designer for Springfield.

racing, they had serious rivals in Excelsior, Merkel and Cyclone. Harley Davidson, who made their first V twin in 1909, did not race themselves, but were happy to advertise the success of private owners. And by about 1912, there were at least 30 well-established makes that almost had the status of household names, in US motorcycle manufacturing.

By that time a pattern had been established. Roads that were atrocious by European standards demanded sturdier frames. Front forks were usually of the bottom link pattern and again very robust. Twist grips were common for controls, with the throttle usually on the left, and piano wires were used rather than the Bowden cable that was ubiquitous in Europe.

Brakes were, if anything, ahead of those in Europe, a popular system being a contracting band and expanding shoes using the same drum on the rear wheel. Similarly, American carburettors, such as the Holley, Schebler and Hedstrom, were definitely ahead of their European counterparts. Much attention was paid to comfort, with large and elaborately suspended saddles and sturdy metal footboards. Spring frames were not common, but when offered, as by Pope, they were of sound design. Europeans found American controls difficult. As noted above, the throttle was usually controlled by the left hand, but so were the gears if any and, often, even the clutch — this might have a lever alongside the left hand side of the tank as well as a foot pedal, also on the left.

Lighting and electrical equipment was generally excellent. The US manufacturers did not make the mistake of depending on Germany for magnetos, and offered electric lighting as standard, long before it was thought of in Europe. Indian, indeed, scored a notable 'first' in 1914 with the all electric 'Hendee special' featuring electric starting! Though this innovation was a failure, costing the company a good deal of money, it illustrates Indian's forward-looking attitude.

As early as 1914, however, economic forces were at work that could not be denied. Quite a few of the pioneer names had already disappeared in the face of determined marketing by Indian, Harley Davidson and Excelsior. Now the appearance of incredibly cheap cars, such as Ford's Model T, was to eat into the sales of motorcycles, so it was no coincidence that, between 1915 and 1918, such well thought of companies as Pope, Yale, Iver Johnson, Cyclone, Thor and Peerless ceased production along with many others. Of those 'household names' a mere half dozen survived into the 1920s and only Indian, Harley Davidson and Excelsior lasted out the decade.

Excelsior — sold in Europe as 'the American X' — had sprung from Ignatz Schwin's bicycle manufacturing company in Chicago in 1908 and during the war years had absorbed the Detroit-built four-cylinder in-line Henderson, which Excelsior were to sell in vastly improved form post-war. In-line fours, indeed, became something of a cult in the USA. They had their origin in the Pierce Arrow of 1909, a free-hand copy of an imported Belgian FN. The Pierce lasted just long enough to inspire the Henderson, first made in 1912. Post war, the Henderson brothers left Excelsior to make the Ace, which, when Bill Henderson was killed in a road accident, passed in due course to Indian. As the Indian Four, it remained in production until the USA entered the Second World War in 1941.

The USA's other highly respected in-line four was the Cleveland, made from 1925 to 1929. All of these were extremely powerful luxurious motorcycles with tireless performance. As much as anything, they exemplified a general US trend in the 1920s towards a super sporting performance that no car — cheap or otherwise — could provide. With a power-to-weight ratio at least three times better than that of a powerful car, US V twins and fours were used in large numbers by the police, the armed forces and, to a lesser extent, by public utilities. They also sold to sporting enthusiasts, the V twins forming the backbone of

Class C Amateur racing in the 1930s. The demands of off-road competition, hill climbing, and long distances on the vastly improved roads of that era resulted in motor-cycles that, to European eyes, soon became grotesquely over-engineered.

Excelsior had dropped out of contention in 1931 to concentrate on bicycles and, for most of the 1930s, Indian and Harley Davidson were on a fairly equal footing in almost every respect. There was one vital difference, how-ever. George Hendee had retired from his Indian company in 1916. Harley Davidson remained firmly in the hands of the families who had started it back in the pioneer days of the 1900s.

The 1930s saw a general stagnation in design, confirmed rather than otherwise by Class C competition, which limited amateur racing to side-valve engines of 750cc. An afterthought in the regulations allowed over-head-valve engines of 500cc, though this remained academic, until Canadian rider Billy Matthews won the 1941 Daytona 200 mile race on a Norton International! The overwhelming popularity of British motor cycles in the USA after the Second World War was a phenomenon that the local industry could never have foreseen. Harley Davidson retrenched — and bought out the Italian Aermacchi company between 1956 and 1960. Indian, however, tried to meet the invasion head on with a totally new Euro-pean-type range, the so-called 'Torque' models, the 220cc (later 250cc) and 440cc (later 500cc) single-cylinder Arrow and ver-tical twin Scout. A 1000cc in-line four was also planned. At this point, the British com-pany J Brockhouse & Co provided a massive capital injection that gave them control, not only of the Indian Sales Corporation, but of manufacturing at Springfield. Losses on the

During the First World War, the American Forces ordered 70,000 Harleys, some rigged as armed outfits (above). Britain had a Clyno-Vickers machine-gun outfit (below).

Torque range forced Brockhouse to suspend manufacture in 1953 and subsequent 'Indians' sold in America were thinly-disguised British models. Indian's long and honourable history was over.

Harley Davidson took a different view of the US market. Arguing that, though lightweights might be popular, there would always be sales for the traditionally rugged style of native motorcycle, they re-designed and updated their big V twins and elevated their ownership into a cult. They were able to use their Italian connection to satisfy the consid-

Historic border-crossing (left) by Harley-Davidson on Armistice Day, 1918. British dispatch-riders used machines by Phelan and Moore, Douglas, BSA, Triumph and others.

erable demand for cheaper and lighter
models with at least an American name,
meanwhile doggedly improving their bigger
and better V twins. The Aermacchi connection was severed in the late 1970s. By that
time, persistance, determination and excellence of management had once again made
Harley Davidson a force to be reckoned with
in the US market. They had survived the
British invasion, the subsequent flooding of
the market by the Japanese and the brief era of
Spanish imports. In the 1980s, indeed, Japanese manufacturers paid Harley Davidson
the ultimate compliment of blatantly copying
their layout and styling! Harley Davidson's
survival — and survival in good health and on
their own terms — is one of the most fasci-
nating episodes in motor cycling's long and
honourable history.

Small-town America, 1910. A Sunday morning
gathering of enthusiasts in Nebraska, about to
set off for a 150-mile jaunt.

The mid-1930s Harley Davidson (left) and
Indian (right), both the product of Class C
amateur racing.

THE 1920s...THE GOLDEN AGE

GOLDEN AGES BECOME so only in retrospect, so no doubt motor cyclists everywhere grumbled just as much about their grievances in the years between the wars as they ever did before, or have done since. Those years, however, definitely saw enormous changes for the better, both in the economic circumstances of the average enthusiast — this was the first time ordinary wage earners found themselves able to afford to buy and run a motor cycle — and in the way motor cycles were designed.

If the average motor cycle of 1939 is compared with that of 1919, the average enthusiast would marvel not so much at the differences but at the improvements. Side valves have given way to overhead versions, which are fully enclosed at that, quietened by a copious circulation of oil that, as a bonus, carries away excessive heat from the cylinder head. The lubrication system itself is vastly improved, with, instead of the arbitrary injection of oil by a simple hand-operated pump, automatic engine-driven pumps circulating it to every vital part and allowing it to cool by returning it to the oil tank. Dubious three-speed gearboxes with clumsy hand change have given way to foolproof four-speed varieties, operated by a foot pedal. Brakes have improved beyond belief. So have tyres, which are now wired onto the rims rather than held on by air pressure. No longer does a deflated tyre roll off the rim in lethal fashion. Transmission belts have been replaced by chains. Even the cheapest lightweight two-stroke has electric lighting, usually with a battery and automatic control that ensures correct charging by the built-in dynamo.

The motor cycle of 1939, therefore, is altogether a more practical affair than its 1919 ancestor. It is easier to clean, too, with lavish user of untarnishable, durable chromium plating in place of nickel, which, unless laboriously polished, dulled to a dirty grey within weeks. Performance has been transformed as well. Between the first post-war Senior TT of 1920 and that of 1939, the speed had risen from the 51.48mph of Tommy de la Hay's side-valve Sunbeam to the staggering 89.38mph of Georg Meier's supercharged double ohc BMW twin.

Such was the universal appeal of motor cycling in these years that, despite local influences and accidents that shaped the designs of one national industry along other lines to those of another, progress was constant, in Europe at any rate. That the same was not true of the USA was not the fault of the US motor-cycle industry.

In fact, the best American motor cycles of 1919 were considerably in advance of most of their European contemporaries. Pre war, the US industry had already standardised the use of countershaft gearboxes, while, in Europe flimsy epicyclic hub gears had been all the rage. Similarly, the USA had gone over to chain drive, while Europe stuck to the belt. The motor cycles themselves were handsome, powerful and robustly made. The factories were superbly equipped, taking advantage of the most up-to-date production methods, which meant that US machines could be shipped across the Atlantic and still sell at competitive prices. They did so in sufficient quantities to panic the British and European domestic industries into demanding that tariff barriers should be erected to half this penetration. This came to pass. For all their vision and efficiency, US manufacturers were abrubtly denied access to an export market that had become vital to them, because cheap cars, a menace before the war, now threatened the very existence of the domestic American motor cycle.

The industry shrank and retrenched, with many of the companies that had survived until now disappearing. The 'big three' — Indian, Harley Davidson and Excelsior (makers of big V twins as well as the superb Henderson four) — were forced to depend on what export markets were left to them, and on sales to the police, the armed forces, pubic utilities, and sportsmen. Excelsior stopped manufacture in the face of the depression in 1931, leaving Indian and Harley Davidson to fight out their bitter rivalry.

The USA's vanishing motor cycle industry was saved in the 1930s by the introduction of Class C Amateur racing, whose regulations specified little more than basically standard production machines with 750cc side-valve engines should be used. Events comprised a strange mix of road racing, enduro runs, TT racing, flat track and speedway contents. TT racing was on a dirt surface, with gradients and left and right turns. Flat track was on loose-surfaced tracks of up to half a mile, while speedway racing took place on longer tracks with steeply banked turns.

Class C was an instant success. After 1937, when Daytona Beach became its focal point, a genuine revival of interest in motor cycles and motorcycling resulted. On the other hand, however, the somewhat restrictive formula and the need for one motor cycle to fulfill so many functions led to stagnation and moved the US motor cycle far away from the concepts of European design.

There was another facet of the US scene, particularly in urban California, that is often forgotten. This was the motor scooter, which cropped up over and over again in the years between the wars. It was one such scooter, an American Autoped, owned by a prominent English member of parliament, that found its way into an article in early 1919 in the *Daily News* and started a craze in Britain that amounted to a mania. The newspaper was swamped with letters, literally by the sackful. A rumour that one London store had Autopeds in stock saw people queuing half way down Oxford Street. The interest spilled over into the motor cycle magazines though, to give them their due, the editorial staff showed little enthusiasm. Every week saw dozens of projected designs, most of them crude and impractical. Many small under-capitalised firms were set up to build scooters and a few actually staggered into production, by which time the mania had subsided. This left concerns such as ABC Skootamota, Kenilworth and Autoglider — high and dry. No wonder that British manufacturers hesitated when Italian and German scooters appeared on the market 30 odd years later.

Curiously, though the craze for scooters did not reach the same height in Germany, it

The post-war years saw a short-lived craze for the scooter (left). The unorthodox 5-cylinder Megola was raced by Toni Bauhofer and reached speeds up to 140 km/h.

lasted longer, and DKW made scooters that at least sold in reasonable numbers. Expatriate Danish engineer J S Rasmussen had founded his DKW company at Zschopan near Chemnitz in Saxony to build steam lorries — Dampe Kraft Wagen — but quickly switched after 1919 to making clip-on auxiliary engines for bicycles, scooters and ultra lightweight motor cycles, all powered by simple two-stroke engines designed by Herman Weber. These engines were also widely sold in Germany to other makers. Though DKW did make larger

machines, favourable tax concessions meant that the vast majority were of 200cc and less.

Somehow, the company managed to survive the appalling hyper-inflation of 1923 that killed off so many other concerns and indeed flourished mightily. They began racing in the 175cc and later 250cc classes with Hugo Ruppe-designed engines, utilising his patented Ladepumpe charging piston below the crankcase. Soon these 'blown' DKWs demanded water cooling to cope with their power. They were extremely successful

in road racing and in the long-distance hill climbs so popular in Germany. However, in Grand Prix racing they were not really a match for the British four-strokes, or, for that matter, the Austrian Puchs, which used a split-single two-stroke engine, also pump-charged.

So soundly were DKW beaten by Puch in the 1930 and 1931 seasons that they called in designer Arnold Zoller, who laid out split-single racing engines — still using the charging piston — that were gradually developed into

'Lawrence of Arabia' (big picture) owned no less than eight Brough-Superior machines. In the bottom picture, from the left, designer and manufacturer George Brough, racer Eddy Meyer and works manager Ike Webb outside the factory in 1927.

the most powerful two-strokes that the world had ever seen. As a result, DKW won the 250cc European championship in 1934, 1935 and 1938 and both the 250cc and 350cc championships in 1939. Perhaps their finest achievement was Ewald Kluge's 1938 Lightweight TT win at over 80mph, a result that convinced even the most sceptical.

Germany's other most celebrated and successful motor cycle between the wars was the BMW, first seen at the Paris Salon of 1923. Originally war-time aircraft engine makers, BMW had embarked on a number of enterprises before starting to manufacture a proprietary flat-twin motor cycle engine. They then decided to make a motor cycle of their own, with shaft drive, so that a transverse engine layout and unit gearbox were natural features to incorporate. Like DKW, BMW raced from an early date with great success and adopted supercharging wholeheartedly. Rider Ernst Herne held the world's fastest record no less than six times in the 1930s, BMW won the 500cc European championship of 1938, and in 1939, riders Georg Meier and Jock West finished first and second in the Senior TT.

Innovative and superbly crafted, the big BMW bikes were very expensive as befitted what were probably the best motor cycles in the world in those years. They did make smaller, somewhat less expensive single-cylinder models of between 200cc and 400cc — still with shaft drive — but exclusivity was BMW's trademark. Next to Britain's, the German industry between the wars was probably the busiest in Europe, despite economically troubled times. Strangely, many firms, by no means obscure concerns, used British engines, gearboxes and other proprietary components. To some extent, this was a tribute to the efficiency of the British industry and its resulting low prices, but it also reflected the esteem in which British motor cycles were held on the continent. JAP, Blackburne, Sturmey Archer (Raleigh) and Python (Rudge) engines were widely used, as were the Bradshaw oil-cooled engine and the remarkable Barr & Stroud sleeve valve. It was a considerable loss to Britain when Adolf Hitler came to power and put an end to this widespread dependence on imported compoents. No less was it a source of embarressment to those German firms left high and dry.

As in Germany, France saw an upsurge of interest in motor cycling immediately after the First World War and a number of imaginative and advanced designs were produced.

Aircraft makers Bleriot and engine manufacturers Gnome et Rhone both saw the mass production of motor cycles as the solution for factories suddenly made idle. The former showed interesting vertical twins, while the latter chose to build the British ABC under licence. Somehow, however, French enthusiasm was short-lived, though the native industry tried hard to keep up with the latest technological developments, this soon became little more than a prestige exercise at the annual Paris Salon. What did sell, and in numbers that kept the industry alive if not exactly flourishing, was the 100cc Velomoteur that was untaxed and could be ridden without even the formality of a driving licence.

Nor was there the sporting interest in France that so sustained motor cycling in Germany. The French Grand Prix turned into an ill-supported and even worse attended farce. The magnificent racing complex built at Montlhery, 20 miles from Paris, never paid its way — though the 1.7-mile banked track was popular for record breaking. Yet, strangely, the 'speed week' at Arpajon, held on a narrow tree-lined stretch of road with a four mile undulating straight, attracted entrants from all over Europe, while the Bol d'Or, an extraordinary 24-hour race with no change of rider, that started in 1924 on a public road circuit in the forest of St Germain near Paris, survived for the next 15 years. The first race was won by an 500cc ohv Sunbeam, victory in it remaining a British preserve, which makes its survival all the more surprising.

Italy was a late comer to motor cycle manufacture, but, as the 1920s wore on, made up for it in full measure. Garelli and Moto Guzzi joined Gilera and Frera as sporting makers, as did Benelli and Bianchi. Italian designers were early and enthusiastic advocates of ohv and ohc engines and the use of light alloy components and soon developed a sense of style that they have never lost.

Racing — especially long-distance open road racing from town to town — became an Italian institution. With the supercharged Rondine — later Gilera — the Italians could justly have claimed to have begun the trend to four-cylinder racing machines. Dorino Serafini's European title on the 500cc Gilera in 1939 was a taste of things to come. Moto Guzzi first raced in the TT in 1926, and in 1935 were rewarded when Stanley Woods won both Lightweight and Senior races. And in 1937 on a Moto Guzzi Omobono Tenni won the Lightweight TT — the first foreign rider ever to win a TT.

Yet, for all their excellence and sporting pedigree, Italian motor cycles were virtually unknown elsewhere in Europe. Given their reputation in racing and in the International Six Days Trial, why the Italians made no attempt to export is hard to understand. Perhaps it was because, as in Germany, taxation encouraged smaller engines, so many of those exquisite Italian ohc models were of 250cc and below.

Without doubt, however, it was the British industry that dominated European motor cycling between the wars. To some extent, this was because it enjoyed a virtually 'captive' colonial export market, particularly in Australia, but there was naturally more to it than that. The concentration of diverse skills and experience in the British Midlands, the intense competition between not only motor cycle manufacturers, but also the makers of proprietary equipment, and the part played by an unsensational and responsible specialist press all played their parts.

Though British design ws perhaps conservative, this may have been no bad thing — evolution is better than revolution, as history seems to show. In addition, many British designers were only too aware of the strange story of the post-war ABC. This wonder motor cycle, with its 400cc ohv flat twin engine set transversely across the frame, unit construction car-type gearbox with gate change by hand lever, self-dumping leaf-spring suspension fore and aft, internal expanding brakes, ingenious frame design and electric lighting with built-in dynamo, embodied everything that a motor cyclist could wish, including generous weather protection.

Designed by the young Granville Bradshaw, the ABC truly appeared to be ten — even 20 — years ahead of its time when it was revealed in prototype form early in 1919. The machine was to be made by the Sopwith aviation and engineering company in a purpose-equipped factory, with a production target of 10,000 a year, but despite the brilliance of the overall concept and Sopwith's money, the ABC was a damaging fiasco. It took 15 months to reach production, only for Sopwith to go into voluntary liquidation after fewer than 2,500 motor cycles had been made. A disappointed British public turned to the next best, which might not be all that much ahead of the times, but which did at least live up to its maker's claims and its reputation.

Such British marques as Sunbeam, Norton,

By the late 1930s, the German BMW, with oil-damped telescopic front forks, was probably the most luxurious motor cycle.

AJS, Scott, BSA and Triumph sold world
wide. British bikes won the TT year after year
and the European Grand Prix races as well.
Britain's dominance of the market extended
beyond the super-sports mould into other
areas as well. There were plenty of companies
using the 270cc Villiers two-stroke engine, or
the small side-valve engines made by JAP or
Blackburne. As in Germany, there were many
'manufacturers' who made little themselves,
assembling their motor cycles almost entirely
from bought-in components. This could be an
expensive method, especially for the smaller
firms who could not bargain quantity against
prices, as could a larger company, such as,
say, OK Supreme. Many small firms, and
quite a few larger ones were under capitalised,
and so did not survive the depression of the
early 1930s. Some, however, flourished. New
Imperial, for instance, began to make their
own engines in the mid 1920s and went on to
introduce their own range of unit construction engines and gearboxes and their own
cantilever spring frames in the 1930s. Vincent HRD became their own engine makers in
the 1930s, as did Excelsior with the famous
Manxman ohc engines, which they took over
when Blackburne stopped making motorcycle engines.

The king of the assemblers was the incom-
parable George Brough, who, working from
his small Nottingham factory, advertised his
Brough Superiors as 'The Rolls Royce of
motor cycles'. Brough always insisted on the
best, was his own head tester and rode his own
machinery in trials and speed events with

great success.

Brough Superiors really were hand-made.
Having ordered one and paid a deposit, cus-
tomers were encouraged to visit the factory
several times to check on progress. On each
visit they were expected to pay a further
installment — a procedure that, on the one
hand, mad the eventual settling of a the final
bill less painful, and, on the other, gave
Brough a healthy cash flow.

Most of Brough's machines used big V twin
JAP (and in later years Matchless) engines,
though he built several 'show stoppers' — a
transverse engined V twin, a narrow angle V
four and an in-line air-cooled four-in-line, it is
doubtful if he had any serious intention of
making any of them. However, he did make a
dozen or so outfits with an 800cc water-
cooled Austin 7 engine, gearbox and shaft
drive, with the final drive unit between closely
two-strokes — entered the market with a
set twin rear wheels. Unfortunately, the outbreak of war in 1939, stopped the develop-

ment of another model that Brough certainly
intended to make. This was the ill-fated
1000cc transverse flat four Golden Dream,
with contra-rotating crankshafts, unit
gearbox and shaft drive. It had been the sensation of the 1938 Motor Cycle Show. If 1920s
were the years of development, the 1930s
were those of consolidation. The depression
of the early 1930s that eliminated many small
companies — and brought changes of ownership to several larger ones — only confirmed
the conviction that sales depended upon
value for money. The resilience of the motor
cycle industry was quite remarkable. The
years between the wars culminated with the
birth of — not a new motor cycle, but a new
style of motor cycle — Edward Turner's
500cc Triumph twin. Nothing new in itself,
the Speed Twin and its super sports version,
the Tiger 100, opened up a whole new pro-
spect. To have been young, to have been able
to buy and run a Triumph Twin in 1937 must
have been exciting indeed! Little did those
lucky few realise what lay ahead not so far in
the future. But that is the way of the world, and
we cannot blame those who experienced
those days — and indeed those who only read
about them — from regarding the years
between the wars as a Golden Age.

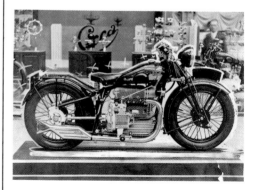

This superb 750cc four-cylinder Moto-became
dates from the late 1930s; the average
Frenchman in the inter-war years, however, was
more likely to be riding the 100cc Velomoteur.

THE STORY OF AN INDUSTRY

THE HISTORY OF ANY long-lived enterprise is shaped by more forces than we usually believe, and the history of the motorcycle industry — and of motorcycles — is no exception.

Foremost — without which there would be no story — was the work of countless individuals. Many of them are now forgotten, though some are remembered, while a few have become legends, but all of them, in whichever country and at whatever time, had to contend with the changing world around them.

Advances in technology, improved materials, new inventions, all had to be taken on board. So did fluctuations in prosperity and the rise and fall of different markets. Changing prices of raw materials — and of petrol — were important. Taxes and tariffs — on imports or exports — could be altered at the stroke of a pen. And industrial strife and unrest could play a major part. These and a thousand other factors over a span of more than 90 years, explain many apparent anomalies.

Early improvements to motorcycles included spray carburettors and high tension magneto ignition, both of which improved reliability beyond belief. Throttle and ignition controls were moved from the tank top to the handlebars and operated by Bowden cables. Automatic inlet valves gave way to mechanical operation. By about 1907, spring front forks were becoming common. Engines were almost all of about 500cc with side valves; larger V twins of up to 1000cc were usually used when a sidecar was to be pulled.

There had been two speed transmissions from a very early date, notabl that designed by Richard Moore of P & M in 1904, but early engines were enormously flexible, and fixed ratio single speed transmission with V belt drive lasted a long time. A belt was light, cheap and gave wonderfully smooth drive without an expensive shock absorber or cush drive. While they might slip in wet weather, belts did not rapidly wear out, from the mud and grit thrown up from water-bound Macadam roads as did exposed chains. Various 'free engine' clutches and variable ratio pulleys were offered from an early date as proprietary fittings; the ingenious Zenith Gradua and Rudge Multi systems of 'infinitely variable' drive prolonged the life of belt drive up to and beyond the First World War.

Brakes in early days were crude. At the front, there was simply a cycle-type stirrup, which nobody used for fear of a front wheel skid on the loose surfaced roads. At the rear,

The scene outside the Rudge depot at the 1911 T.T. Victor Surridge (nearest camera) was killed during a crash in practice shortly after this — the first T.T. fatality.

there was a shoe that wedged into the belt drive rim. But except in cities, traffic was almost unbelievably sparse.

Such was the general state of the motorcycle in Britain and Europe in about 1907. In that year, there were two innovations that were to affect the British industry enormously and help to make it the strongest in Europe by 1914. the 2¾-mile banked track at Brooklands was opened. Subsequently, this was to prove a testing ground that played a valuable role for over 30 years until it was closed for ever by the outbreak of war in 1939. Of even more importance was the Tourist Trophy race in the Isle of Man. Racing in Europe had lost its way since open road events had been banned after the catastrophic Paris-Madrid race of 1903. The main European event, the International Cup, was an ill conceived farce that was not even spectacular, for only three entries were allowed from each country.

Nor did International Cup regulations do anything to spur development of real motorcycles, for engines of unlimited size were allowed with no fuel consumption limits, whilst at the same time, total weight had to be under 110 lb. Cheating, too, was endemic. British riders, disgusted by the 1906 fiasco, approached the Auto Cycle Club of Britian, and the result was the TT.

The Auto Cycle Union, as it had become by 1907, framed regulations year by year that really did 'improve the breed'. Run at first on the 14-odd mile St John course, the race proved a real test and speeds and reliability improved year by year.

The winning speed rose from 38mph in 1907 to over 50mph in 1910. The ACU then — to encourage development of change speed gears — moved the race to the 37½ mile Mountain circuit, which, slightly altered in 1920 to 37¾ miles and improved beyond belief over many years, is still in use today. European manufacturers took part from the start, while, by 1911, such was the TT's prestige that Indian came all the way from the USA to compete — and were rewarded by a 1-2-3 Senior win. This was a shock to British pride, but it was to be a further 24 years before there was another foreign victory.

The outbreak of war in 1914 had little influence on either the industry or on design, though the drying-up of German supplies meant that the making of magnetos had to developed. A few radical post-First World War designs, notably the transverse twin ABC, excited much interest, but the ABC died of slapdash hasty design and the ineptitude of its sponsors — the wartime airframe makers, Sopwith.

Countershaft gearboxes and chain drive — both pioneered by Indian (and made acceptable by their TT win) took over in the early 1920s and gearbox manufacture became another speciality.

Proprietary engine makers fought each

other to a standstill that soon left JAP and Blackburne the survivors with some opposition from the oil-cooled Bradshaw and the unique sleeve valve Barr & Stroud. 'Assembled' motor cycles flourished, their builders making nothing themselves, but buying in engines, frames, gearboxes, wheels, tanks, saddles and other components from the huge infrastructure that had developed. Villiers of Wolverhampton became suppliers of proprietary two-stroke engines to the world. Nor were British exports confined to its empire. Germany became so dependent upon the British industry that by 1930, purchases of engines, gearboxes and other components reached a value exceeded only by exports of complete motor cycles to Australia.

Italy too, was a good customer, for the Italian industry was a late starter. Sunbeam, Norton, AJS and other sporting British machines had a ready sale there. So, too, was France, where the native industry took an easy option, largely making a living from 'Velomoteurs' of 100cc that sold for not much more than the price of a bicycle and needed no road tax, licence or insurance.

Between the wars, the motorcycling world believed that British was best, even though good, even great motorcycles were being made elsewhere. Germany's BMW and DKW, Belgium's FN and Switzerland's Motosacoche, Italy's Gilera and Moto Guzzi, were all excellent makes as were many more. But between the wars, Britain undoubtedly led the world. America's early promise had faded with the success of Henry Ford's Model T. With the Tin Lizzie costing less than a good

motorcycle, only the market for heavy, large capacity high performances bikes was left, exemplified by Indian and Harley Davidson. As American design became introverted and the machines ever bigger and heavier, it lost its appeal in other markets.

After the Second World War, a policy of austerity and petrol rationing at home meant that the British bought mainly utility 125cc and 197cc two-strokes, but the industry set to with a will to sell, to America sporting 500cc and later 600cc and 650cc machines modelled on Triumph's successful pre-war Speed Twin. However, unknowingly, the British industry had entered an era of stagnation. For the moment, it was too easy. Even the dreary little two-strokes found export buyers in their tens of thousands, but, over the next dozen years or so, these markets, most of them in 'empire' countries, were to contract and disappear behind trade barriers favourable to them, but not to the British. Eventually, the only real overseas market left was the USA. The actual home market shrank too — far too much to support the whole industry. A second-hand car rather than a sidecar outfit became the working man's transport. With the appearance of the Austin Morris Mini, the ordinary motor cycle was doomed.

The British industry, with its eye on the USA, seemed particularly inept over the one area that was left in the home market. The appearance of 50cc mopeds from Germany and Italy produced no response. BSA had made a dreadful job of the clever, but flawed, BSA Dandy, while their 75cc Beagle and the 50cc Ariel Pixie scarecely saw production.

Thus, the Japanese — in particular Honda — from a vast and protected home market, were able to penetrate Britain at a level that the domestic manufacturers hardly acknowledged as existing.

When Honda launched their four cylinder 750cc CB750 in the USA in 1969, it gave the British a mortal blow. In an era of high taxation and dreadful labour relations, the BSA company made some terrible blunders and with the ill fated 350cc BSA Fury and Triumph Bandit twins, missed the market entirely for the 1972 season. The Japanese moved in for the kill, and the rest is history.

When the late Erwin Tragatsch first compiled this monumental work, he lamented the still recent facts. 'The saddest story of all', he called the death of the British industry with which he had been so well acquainted. He blamed bad management — of which in later years there had been more than enough. But he also blamed bad government — a point often overlooked by commentators with no experience of business. Yet could anything have saved British motor cycles? Probably not, in view of the shrinking home market, except protectionist policies which no British government would countenance. Germany's proud and confident industry largely collapsed in the late 1950s because of overproduction, rising domestic affluence, the

Inside the machine shop of an early motor cycle factory. Though the actual bikes have changed dramatically, manufacturing methods have not altered that substantially; contrast this picture of a modern Japanese plant with the previous one, which dates from the turn of the century.

The Honda CB750 four-cylinder 'superbike'
(below) ended the dominance of large British
machines in America. Bottom: Two
motorcycling milestones — the 50cc NSU
Quickly moped (left) and the tiny Honda
'stepthrough' (right) that emerged a decade
later.

appearance of cheap cars and failure to export. Italy's industry was horribly weakened at the same time by labour troubles and, though the Italians did adopt a protectionist attitude, much of what is left of their industry has entered the 1990s in very indifferent health.

It is easy to forget that for roughly 25 years there was a flourishing Spanish industry with quite remarkable export sales to the USA. It was hampered — and yet at the same time protected — by the Franco regime's insistence on self sufficiency, and export successes were largely based on the low Spanish labour costs of the time. But when Spain again became part of the European community, its industry was as vulnerable as any to the Japanese.

Worldwide, sales of motor cycles have dropped to such a low total figure that the output of one vigorous and extremely efficient industry, the Japanese, can satisfy the entire demand. In fact it can more than satisfy it, and signs are that even the Japanese industry is suffering from over-production.

Attempts both in Britain and elsewhere to establish a sort of 'bespoke' motor cycle industry — selling expensive hand made machines of individualistic design have met with various difficulties. A few have been minimally successful. Some more ambitious ventures, such as Hesketh, have been failures. It would be unfair and premature to apply that epithet to the rotary engined Norton, but that company has had an uphill struggle. John Bloor's brave attempt to revive Triumph is too young to be judged.

In Britain at any rate, successive legislation has, in the 1990s, made it harder and harder to become a motor cyclist at all, and at the end of 1991, draconian rises in the cost of insurance look like accelerating motor cycling's decline.

In astonishing contrast is the interest of Britain and Europe in the 'classic movement' which was focussed by the publication in the late 1970s of the magazine *Classic Bike* and which has gathered momentum ever since. A whole new industry has arisen to service this interest. Perhaps one day from this will come a new motorcycle industry — who knows? Stranger things have happened as the 20th century enters its last decade.

Many different manufacturers supplied machines for military use. American M.P.s used the Harley-Davidson; BMW supplied their R35 (below) and R75 (right). Bottom: BSA were one of the major British suppliers, making both 350 and 500cc models. The Indian soldier is reclining on a Matchless G3/L, a 350cc ohv machine.

THE GREAT DESIGNERS

PERHAPS the first really famous design, if only because it was so bold, was Paul Kelecom's FN four-cylinder-in-line of 1904. At first of only 400cc, it had shaft drive but neither clutch nor gears. It was rapidly improved and enlarged, gained a clutch and gears and not only sold extensively in its native Belgium, but was exported to England and America. The first American 'in-line-four', the Pierce Arrow, was an acknowledged copy of an imported FN and started a tradition that embraced Henderson, ACE, Excelsior, Cleveland and Indian. The FN 4, latterly of 750cc and with chain final drive, was made until 1926. Nor was this Kelecom's only successful design.

In England, Alfred Scott virtually reinvented the Day-cycle (crankcase compression) two-stroke engine, developing it over several years into a small twin suitable for a motorcycle. First offered for sale in 1909, the 'two speed, two cylinder, two stroke' Scott was a design of remarkable integrity that sold steadily until the end of the 1920s. Indeed the engine layout lasted into the 1960s.

The air-cooled single-cylinder Levis two-stroke, designed by Howard (Bob) Newey and the Butterfield half-brothers, was the first downright practical and uncomplicated lightweight. It first appeared in 1911, became enormously successful and was the basis of Levis two-strokes until 1939. It was also very widely imitated and made under licence. The German Zundapp company paid it a wonderful compliment in 1921 when they copied it to the smallest detail — without acknowledgement. They subsequently copied Levis model changes year by year until 1926.

No such copying was involved in the Velocette two-stroke of 1913, designed by Percy Goodman. Velocette, too, continued to make excellent two-strokes until the Second World War. Goodman also designed the immortal overhead camshaft K series of Velocettes, which first appeared in 1925, and later, the 'high camshaft' series of MOV, MAC and MSS — 250cc, 350cc and 500cc. The 500cc Velocetter 'Thruxton' was still in production in 1970 — a design life of 37 years.

Other long-lived designs include the horizontal single-cylinder layout of Carlo Guzzi's Moto Guzzi of 1921, Adalberto Garelli's side-by-side split-single two-stroke of 1933 and Giovanni Marcellino's fore-and-aft split single Puch (with asymmetrical port timings) that stayed in production in one model or another from 1923 until the late 1960s.

However, very rarely is a design really and truly 'original'. Edward Turner is often credited with having 'invented' the even-firing vertical twin with his Triumph Speed Twin of 1937. This is nonsense. There had been dozens of such twins in the past, while Triumph themselves had made the 650cc Val Page designed 6/1 twin since 1933, and even that was probably inspired by designs by Herman Reeb that Horex in Germany had launched a year earlier as 600cc and 800cc ohc models for sidecar use. But Turner's 1937 design, though in no way radical, was so remarkably neat and compact, so simple to produce, and had such a good all-round performance, that it set a style that was to be copied by all. Development of Turner's design in its various versions, lasted for more than 40 years.

Turner, in fact, had earlier been responsible for another design that really did show originality — the 500cc overhead camshaft Ariel Square Four that was the sensation of the 1930 Motor Cycle Show. Its unique cylinder layout and coupled contra-rotating crankshafts were never copied in its lifetime, its production life spanning nearly thirty years. Its capacity was raised to 600cc and then, with a complete redesign, to 1000cc. Brilliant designer as he was, Turner proved an even greater success as a manager at Triumph, where his career was legendary.

Nothing like so flamboyant as Turner, though equally deserving of being remembered as a designer, was Val Page, who joined JAP in 1914 and, after the war, revitalised their range of engines before leaving in 1925 to join Ariel. Once again he laid down a series of designs that put Ariel on a par with any other manufacturer of the time. He helped Turner with the square four and then went to Triumph. There, he designed the 250cc, 350cc and 500cc range of ohv singles later restyled by Turner as the Tiger 70, Tiger 80 and Tiger 90 models. As earlier mentioned, he also designed the 650cc 6/1 twin. In 1936, Page moved to BSA, where again he drew up a range of eminently modern single cylinder engines, which included the original M23 Gold Star. He moved back to Ariel in 1939. His last design for them was the brilliant all-enclosed 250cc twin-cylinder Ariel Leader two-stroke and its sporting version, the Arrow. Very few designers in any country can have been so prolific and successful.

In 1919, J S Rasmussen's DKW factory in Saxony set Germany on the road to supremecy in the manufacture of two strokes between the wars. Original designs by Hugo Ruppe were developed and then superseded by those of Herman Weber. In 1931, the Swiss-born designer Arnold Zoller was called in to develop split-single DKW racing

Three great designers — Val Page (left), Bert Hopwood (right) and Edward Turner (centre) — photographed at Triumph in 1937.

George William Patchett (left) of McEvoy, FN and Jawa and Walter William Moore of Douglas, Norton and NSU.

machines with water cooling and piston-pump assisted (blown) induction. With patient development by August Prussing, the 'blown' DKW became insuperable in the 250cc class in European road racing in the 1930s.

Unlike Puch, whose Marcellino designed and developed racers had inspired DKW to call in Arnold Zoller, DKW did not sell split-single two-strokes for road use. Instead, they became the first in the world to market 'flat-top piston' two-strokes, using the Schnurle patents. Herman Weber was again the designer. His RT125 of 1937 set entirely new standards of two-stroke performance.

However, the RT125's extraordinary claim to fame was that its design was copied post-war by BSA for their 125cc Bantam, by Harley Davidson, by JL0, by Yamaha, by Suzuki and by at least another half dozen firms in Russia and Eastern Europe. It even formed the basis of post war DKW and MZ racing machinery when Germany was re-admitted to international competition. Under the control of race chief Walter Kaaden, MZ went on to develop the first two-strokes to equal and then to surpass the specific power outputs of four-stroke engines. Today's all conquering racing two-strokes all derive from Kaaden's work at MZ.

Walter Moore designed a 500cc ohc racing engine for Norton, which won the 1927 Senior TT on its first outing. Thereafter, though, it proved disappointing, so when Moore left to join NSU in Germany and to design a similar engine for them, Norton's Joe Craig breathed over young Arthur Carroll's shoulder as he designed a new engine for 1931 – with which Tim Hunt that year 'did the double', winning both Junior and Senior TTs. So was born the Manx Norton, which in the next 18 seasons, was to win 28 TTs, not to mention uncounted Grand Prix races, quite apart from its myriad successes in the hands of private owners right into the 1960s and even beyond.

In post-war Italy, Giulio Carcano attained legendary stature with his designs and development for the Moto Guzzi racing team between 1948 and 1957, his masterpiece being the celebrated 500cc V8. But one Moto Guzzi design of that era, the 500cc in-line watercooled four-cylinder with shaft drive, raced in 1953 and 1954, was designed not by Carcano, but by Carlo Giannini. He, together with Pietro Remor, had been involved long before the war with the four-cylinder design that became the watercooled supercharged Rondine, later taken over by Gilera for the 1937 season.

Post war, Remor was to design first the 1947 air cooled 500cc four-cylinder Gilera, and then in 1950, the very similar four-cylinder MV. Credit for developing the Gilera must go to Franco Pasoni, and that for the MV to Arturo Magni. Remor left MV in 1953 and joined the obscure company Motom. But between 1958 and 1974, MV won the 500cc world championship no less than 17 times.

One cannot leave Italian designers without mentioning Moto Guzzi's Antonio Miccuchi, while Fabio Taglioni of Ducati will always be remembered for his desmodromic valve gear, first used in 1958. Until very recently, his advanced designs kept Ducati right at the forefront of the field with medium-to-large-capacity sporting twins.

Remor (left) with Gilera

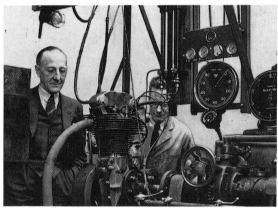

Joe Craig supervises a Manx Norton engine test. He was the architect of Norton's racing success for 25 years.

Fabio Taglioni (above) designed the Ducati desmodromic valve gear in the early 1960s. The system is still in use. Right: Giulio Carcano with Moto-Guzzi Junior TT winner in 1956.

Jack Williams, chief development engineer on the AJS 7R, with son-in-law Tom Herron, of Yamaha

Pioneer Max Friz . . . he made aircraft engines, then the first BMW motorcycle

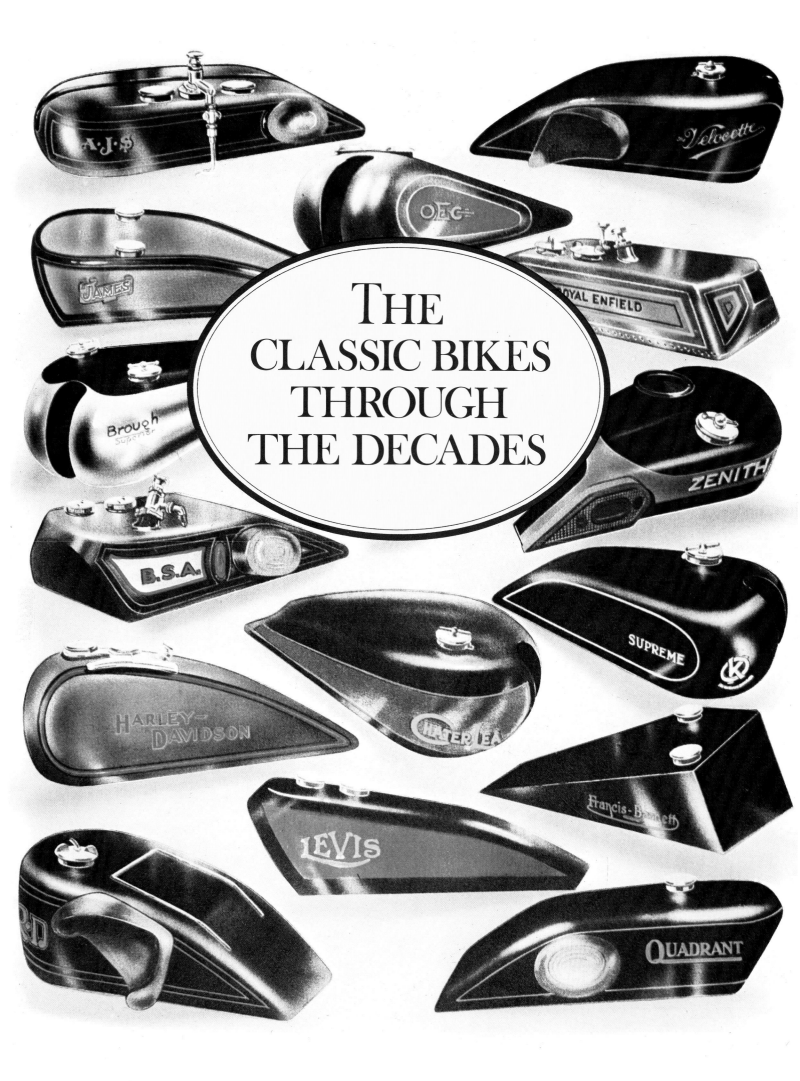

THE
CLASSIC BIKES
THROUGH
THE DECADES

NO FOUR-CYLINDER MOTORCYCLE has achieved such pre-eminence in its own time as the Henderson. It provided riders in the early years of motorcycling with simple starting, smoothness, silence, oil tightness, reliability and generous power to a degree unmatched elsewhere. The model shown here is that of 1912, the first year of production. The original 7 hp model was soon further developed, with a multi-speed gearbox, improved power, and more robust construction. Sales rose accordingly, and the model achieved greater popularity than any comparable machine in the United States. Finally, Ignaz Schwinn's Excelsior Company bought the firm in 1917, initially retaining the services of founders William and Tom

Henderson. After that, the Henderson big four also incorporated the name Excelsior on the tank. Two years later, William and Tom Henderson left Excelsior, unhappy with the new business arrangement. William founded his own motorcycle company, under the name of Ace. He was soon manufacturing an Ace four, and challenging the Henderson's reputation for quality. After many successful years Ace ran into financial troubles, and was bought by Indian.

THE NAME SCOTT is central to the history of the motorcycle. Alfred Scott was an inventor and engine-designer who played a leading part in the development of the two-stroke machine. Scott built his first motorised bicycle in Yorkshire as early as 1898, using a twin-cylinder two-stroke. The engine was fitted to a heavy pedal-cycle, and transmission was by friction roller. By 1903, he had built a machine with rear-wheel power, and a year later Scott was granted British patent rights on a two-stroke vertical-twin engine. Scott's first true production motorcycle was manufactured in 1908. Its engine was built to the Scott design by the nearby Jowett car factory, another Yorkshire concern famous in automotive history. This 333cc engine had a bore and stroke of 58 × 63mm, and the entire unit weighed only 371 lbs. The cylinder heads were water-cooled through a thermosiphon system, but the barrels were air-cooled. By 1914, Scott had settled the design of his machines, and was using a wholly water-cooled engine. The two-speed machine had standard gear-ratios of 3:1 and 4:1, and the unusual "open" frame design which characterised the marque. This frame design was popular with women motorcyclists, whose dignity it helped preserve. Telescopic front forks were used from the very first, and a disc-valve induction and exhaust system was introduced at an early stage. Other machines could match the Scott's 55 mph top speed, but none of its contemporaries offered the same handling qualities. It was this characteristic in particular which afforded Scott such great racing success. Like most unconventional machines, the Scott was the creature of its designer. Alfred Scott himself left the company after the First World War, and died in 1923; within four or five years, the marque had lost much of its shine. Production since a takeover in 1950 has been limited to small-scale revivals. The Scott shown here is a 486cc model specially reconstructed for vintage racing.

INDIAN WAS WITHOUT DOUBT one of the foremost names in the development of the modern motorcycle. In 1905, the factory became one of the first to put a V-twin into commercial manufacture. The first V engine was little more than a doubling up of two Indian 1·75 hp singles, but improved and enlarged versions soon followed. These ultimately provided the basis for the very advanced motorcycles produced under the aegis of the factory's founder, George Hendee, and the great designer Oskar Hedström. After they had left the company, Charlie Gustafson became Indian's chief designer in 1915. He established the side-valve style which became a tradition of the factory and of the American motorcycle industry. His great machine

was the 7 hp 998 cc Power Plus shown here. This sophisticated and speedy motorcycle included such advanced equipment as leaf-spring suspended pivoted fork rear suspension, all chain drive, electric lighting, electric starting and a proper kick-start.

Indian

AS THE ORIGINAL William Brough motor-cycle company entered the last year of its life, the son's rival firm launched the most famous machine to bear the family name. The Brough Superior SS100, introduced in 1925 was more popular than any other prestige sports roadster before or since. The SS100, shown here, was an overhead-valve V-twin. It became one of the two mainstays of Brough Superior's 19-year production period, along with its predecessor, the SS80 side-valve V-twin. As with all engines of its type, the side-valve twin was less durable at speed than the ohv. The '100' and '80' model designations referred to the machines' guaranteed top speed. Brough Superior was also known for a proliferation of multi-cylindered exotica.

The machines were largely assembled from proprietary components — the engines were principally JAP or Matchless units, and even the famous Castle forks were originally a Harley Davidson design. This philosophy was the Achilles' heel of Brough Superior.

The company tried unsuccessfully to develop its own power-units, and the cost of buying-in specially-manufactured engines in small quantities eventually proved to be crippling. The company stopped motor-cycle production in 1940.

Brough Superior

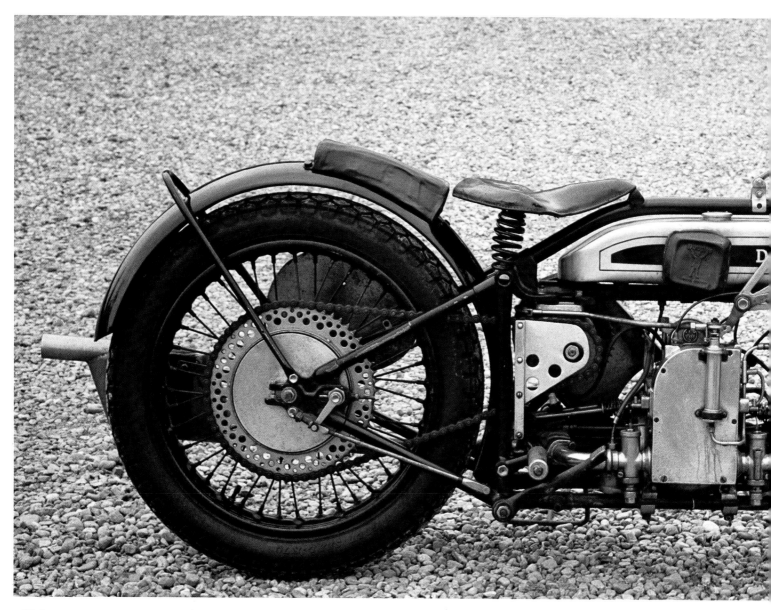

SUNBEAM

THE SUNBEAM MODEL 90, shown on the right in its traditional black-and-gold livery, is probably the finest example of British single-cylinder engineering. It used simple, proven designs, with meticulous finish. The machine was conceived in 1923 as a sports roadster, and successfully adapted as a works racer. It was produced in both 350 and 500cc ohv versions. Production standards dropped after the factory was bought in 1930 by ICI (Imperial Chemical Industries). Sunbeam was later owned by Associated Motorcycles and BSA.

Douglas

ALTHOUGH DOUGLAS did sometimes use other engine layouts, the marque was always known for its horizontally-opposed twins. Today, Douglas is usually re-membered for its post-war series of transverse-engined 350cc machines, but these were only made in the company's last seven years. In its earlier days, and for more than three decades, Douglas found its fame and fortune in exceptionally well-planned twins with a fore-and-aft arrange-ment. The success of these machines owed much to the work of the company's chief development rider, Freddie Dixon, during the middle and late 1920s. Fate also played a part. When the Douglas EW series of 350sv racers began to find the competition tough, Douglas had planned a new ohc model, but a fire at the works destroyed the blueprints and set back the company's work. The new engine was abandoned, and the company chose instead to give a new life to its old ohv twins, with considerable development work by Dixon. By happy chance, these machines proved most successful in the newly-arrived sport of speedway. Some of their success was due to a freak of design which led the frame to flex during broadsliding, but their achievements on the cinder track boosted all aspects of the Douglas reputation. During this period, the classic Douglas machine was the model FW, which was produced in 500cc and 600cc versions. The road-racing version is shown here. The road-racing models were capable of 90 mph and 95 mph respectively. In 1929 alone, 1300 machines were sold.

Rudge

SOME OF THE BEST British production bikes were replicas of their makers' works racing models. A fine example was the 1929 Rudge-Whitworth Ulster, which came from a factory famous for its advanced ap-proach. The machine was introduced to celebrate Graham Walker's win in the Ulster Grand Prix, and it proved to be exceptionally fast and reliable. It had a four-speed positive-stop, foot-change gear-box, dry sump lubrication with a mech-anical pump, and a four-valve cylinder head in a penthouse combustion chamber.

THE BRITISH EXCELSIOR company is re-membered with affection for a 250cc single which was popularly known as the "Mechanical Marvel," but this four-valve ohv machine suffered from its own complexity. Undaunted, Excelsior continued along the same development path with an improved four-valver, the famous Manxman, shown here. This machine had a single overhead camshaft, and each inlet valve was fed by its own Amal RN carburettor. The bronze head, as shown, improved thermal efficiency in the days before aluminium had come into common use. The Manxman shown is a 250, but a 350 was also produced. Valve gear and carburettor tune still proved "very pernickerty" according to Excelsior's managing director Eric Walker, and in 1938 the firm introduced two-valve engines. These were equally fast, but wholly reliable. They had sprung frames, and proved so successful that they continued to be raced in private hands into the early 1950s.

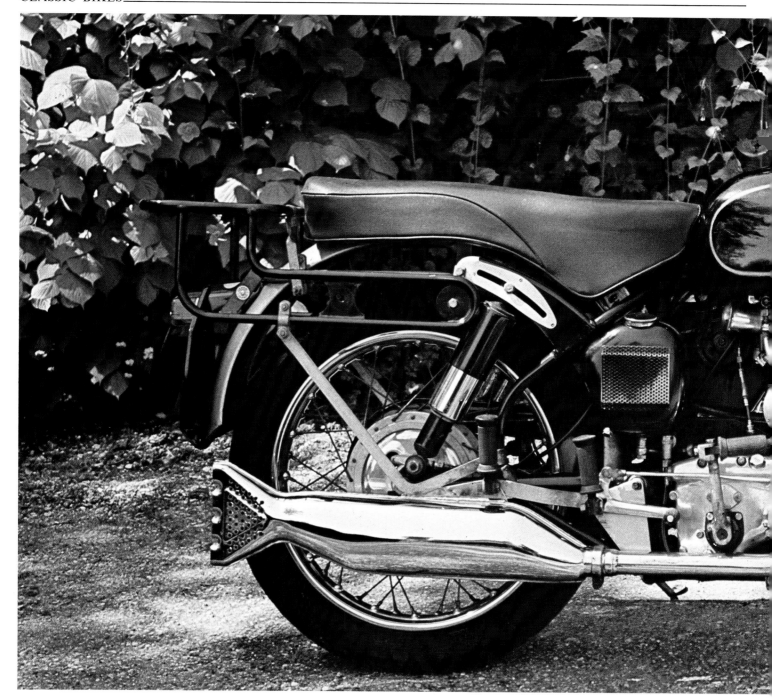

Velocette

OTHER SINGLE-CYLINDER machines may have exemplified a particular aspect of engineering or of performance, but those produced by Velocette demonstrated the full range of attributes. This was best accomplished by the KTT (left), a racing replica of the works' own grand prix machinery, which was also notable as the first model to sport the Velocette-perfected foot gear-change system. This was an ohc

single of 350cc, sold with a guaranteed top speed of 85 mph. As an option, Velocette offered a 100 mph dope-tuned model sporting a 9:1 compression ratio. The range ran from the 1929 Mk 1 illustrated here to the 1949 Mk VIII. In 1956, Velocette demonstrated its skills with a quite different range of well-remembered singles. These were ohv sports roadsters. First came the 499cc Venom, shown above, with a "square" (86 × 86mm) engine, then the smaller 349cc Viper. The Venom engine developed 36 bhp at 6,200 rpm, giving the machine a top speed of 95 mph. After 12 and 24-hour records had been set at Montlhéry, a highly-tuned version was produced as a clubman racer. This was the Thruxton (right), which had a top speed of approximately 120 mph.

BSA

FOR MOST OF ITS LIFE, the BSA marque was known primarily for singles of simple and inexpensive design, made for everyday transport. The motorcycles in the small picture are examples: a 250cc machine from 1925 (background) and the 1928 "Sloper". In later years, the same qualities of durability and reliability were showcased in a much more exotic motorcycle, the Gold Star. No clubman racer has ever enjoyed the success or reputation of the "Goldie". The range was produced in trial, scramble, touring and racing versions, and a 1959 model of the latter is shown here. The 500cc engine developed up to 40 bhp at just over 7,000 rpm, through a close ratio gearbox. Top speed was around 120 mph in full clubman trim.

HARLEY–DAVIDSON

THE HARLEY-DAVIDSON Electra-Glide has its origins in the SV 74 twin of 1922, although its more recent and direct ancestor is the first ohv 1200 of 1941. These early machines displayed the familiar styling features of most American motorcycles: leading link front forks, solid rear wheel mounting, pan saddles, footboards, high, wide handle-bars, and a V-twin engine, all of which produce comfort at low cruising speeds. Over the years, the range has been modernised and renamed, but the essential concept has remained the same. In 1949, the Hydra-Glide was introduced with a telescopic front fork. The next model, with pivoted-fork rear suspension, produced in 1959, was the Duo-Glide. With the addition of a starter motor in 1965 came the name Electra-Glide. Since then, little has changed except the adoption of cast alloy wheels, although numerous Japanese components, such as forks and carburettor, have been adopted. The Electra-Glide is the heaviest mass-produced motorcycle ever built, weighing 800 lbs fully equipped. The 45°, 1207cc V-twin has hydraulically-activated push-rods and produces 62 bhp at 5,200 rpm, and 70ft/lbs of torque at 4,000 rpm. The XLCR (below, kitted out for the track) has similarly won cult status among the world's army of Harley fanatics. The classic sporting Harley, the XLCR was launched in 1976; it is the fastest production bike Harley-Davidson have ever built, with a flat out top speed of a good 120mph. What this, and subsequent Harleys are about — currently the regular 1340cc Evolution series engines are fitted to a range of 17 different bikes — is big vee-twin power, image and style.

THERE ARE MANY REASONS for celebrating the famous marque founded by Howard R. Davies (hence its original name, HRD) and bought shortly afterwards by Philip Vincent. Modern motorcycle manufacturers have still barely caught up with the progressive chassis-group designs produced by Vincent 35 years ago, though the marque is more commonly remembered for its spree of speedy achievement during the 1950s. Perhaps these sporting feats were the inspiration for the unusually-large and ambitious speedo which was fitted to Vincent motorcycles. Factory and private riders captured national and world speed and sprint records by the

handful on the competition model of the period, the Black Lightning. The word "Black" featured in the names of several famous Vincent machines. One unsupercharged Black Lightning achieved a speed of 185·15 mph in the hands of Russell Wright, a New Zealander, in 1955. Sadly, this was also the last year of full production.

The firm went out in a blaze of glory, with the announcement of the semi-streamlined Series D models, but few were actually made. In design, these machines were the natural successors to the Series C Rapides, which had been launched in 1949, with 50-degree 998cc V-twin engines. The Series C standard touring machine provided a top speed of approximately 105/110 mph, and its sporting counterpart the Black Shadow (shown here) went to 110/120 mph, reaching 56 mph in only six seconds. These machines were in turn developed from the Series A Rapides, which were launched in 1937, had 47-degree engines, and had a web of external pipes.

ARIEL was in every sense an historic British marque. Established since 1898, the firm exhibited all the characteristics of British motorcycle manufacture. The products were well made, even sporty, but initially of conventional design. In 1929, a much more sophisticated machine made a considerable break with tradition. This was a 500cc four with a highly-unusual "square" cylinder configuration and single overhead camshaft. This distinctive engine layout became so identifiable with the marque that the nickname "Squariel" passed into the language of motorcycling. Like the later Triumph Speed Twin, another pace-setting machine, the Square Four was designed by Edward Turner. It had an all ball-and-roller bearing engine and horizontally-split crankcase. In 1931, the engine was bored out from 51 to 56 mm, thus increasing capacity to 600cc. Although some modest success was achieved in competition, such as the Bickel brothers' supercharged 111·42 lap at Brooklands in 1934, the machine was really a sporting tourer. In 1936, Ariel launched a 1,000cc Square Four of quite new engine design. This model had a pushrod power-unit, with plain bearings, and it also utilised a unique trailing-link rear-suspension system. It remained in production in various roadster forms until the late 1950s, by which time it boasted four individual exhaust-pipes ports and an all-aluminium engine. The 1956 luxury roadster shown here develops 42 bhp at 5,800 rpm, providing a top speed of 105 mph. It has a bore and stroke of 65 × 75 mm. The machine's kerb-weight is 495 lbs.

TRIUMPH

TRIUMPH WILL ALWAYS be associated with the vertical-twin engine-layout. This classic design was introduced in 1938, in the 498cc Speed Twin, which was the fore-runner of many famous motorcycles. A memorable example was the larger Thunderbird (above), introduced in 1949. This 649cc tourer produced 34 bhp at 6,000 rpm on a compression ratio of 7:1. Three standard models averaged 101·06 mph between them for 500 miles at Montlhéry. A total break with the vertical-twin layout came in the 1960s with the transverse three-cylinder Trident (left). The T160 had a 740cc engine of 67 × 70 mm bore and stroke, giving 58 bhp at 7,250 rpm to reach a top speed of around 120 mph. Production ended in the mid-1970s.

Norton

IT WAS THE GREAT racing success of the Norton marque which created the need for an improved frame in the 1940s. The need was met by the McCandless brothers' Featherbed frame, which in turn influenced motorcycle design almost everywhere. After being introduced on the Manx racers, the Featherbed frame was modified for road use in the existing 497cc tourer, which became the Dominator in 1952. The example shown above is a Manx built in 1958. Ten years after its launch, the Dominator had grown to 647cc, with a maximum road speed of 112 mph. In 1965, Norton launched the 745cc Atlas, but a more significant development came two years later. The same engine was fitted, with rubber mountings, into a new duplex frame. This new model, the Commando, was subsequently increased in size to 828cc. With a top speed of 120 mph, the Commando (bottom) is the most powerful road-going Norton ever produced.

LIKE THE LAMBORGHINI CAR, the equally exotic Laverda is the product of an Italian agricultural engineering group. With its race-bred frame and sleek styling, the 130 mph RGS 1000 (below) is Laverda's flagship. It is derived from the Laverda Jota, which with a top speed of 150 mph verified in independent tests, was the fastest production roadster ever built. The RGS 1000 is powered by a 981cc three-cylinder motor which features 120° crankshaft and gives 80 bhp.

THE MV AGUSTA AMERICA is arguably the finest sports roadster in production, and without doubt a classic among the multi-cylindered big bikes. The entire power-unit is a development of the company's racing 500cc four of the 1950s. MV was the last European marque to dominate the Grand Prix circuits, and retired solely for commercial reasons, but it took several attempts before the factory's sporting experience could be translated into a successful roadster. The 788cc dohc America develops 75 bhp at 8,500 rpm, and its top speed is approximately 135 mph.

MOTO GUZZI

WHILE JAPANESE motorcycles have become increasingly sophisticated, the largest of the Italian manufacturers has responded by offering machines of comparable performance but robust simplicity. The V 850 GT of 1972 typifies Moto Guzzi's approach. The transverse twin turns out 64·5 bhp at a mere 6,500 rpm, providing a top speed of 115 mph. In 1975, the entire range was expanded to include the revolutionary V 1,000, with hydraulic torque converter.

DUCATI

IT WAS BUILT for its high-speed handling, apparently with no other priority in mind, and in this respect the Ducati Desmo 864cc of 1975 has no serious rival. Its top speed is 135 mph, its kerb weight a mere 428 lbs, and it is a remarkably stable motorcycle. The machine also benefits from the efficiency and reliability of the desmodromic valve system. Only Ducati has used this system with total success. The technique was employed to great effect in the 1972 750 SS clubman racer, after being first introduced by the factory's chief engineer, Fabioni Taglioni, in the successful Grand Prix period which was during the late 1950s.

BMW PREACHED THE virtues of conservatism in motorcycle design for decades, preferring to rely on tried and tested engineering, rather than embark on innovation for innovation's sake. The flat twin concept, for long favoured by the company, dated back to the 1930s, for instance; the R100RS (main picture), the classic BMW of the mid-1970s onwards, changed relatively little over the years. Though aerodynamically the machine was very advanced — the result of concentrated fairing development involving elaborated wind tunnel testing — the engine was a practical and simple horizontally-opposed 980cc ohv twin, producing 70bhp at 7,000 rpm and a top speed of around 125mph. Contrast this with the revolutionary K1 (inset), which BMW launched in 1989. This striking, sensa-

tional looking machine was designed to meet and beat the Japanese competition. Its distinctive bodywork is designed for absolute aerodynamic efficiency, while its engine is an improved 16-valve version of the four-cylinder K100 engine of 1984. The combus- tion chambers were reworked and the crankshaft, con rods and pistons lightened, so the unit revved harder, while the machine also utilises the Bosch Motoronic digital engine management system, as fitted to BMW cars. Top speed is 149mph.

THE CBR1000 (main picture) is Honda's flagship sports roadster. Launched in 1987, the machine triumphantly fulfills the brief Honda gave its designers — to produce a 1000cc open class sports bike for the road rider that was powerful, comfortable and smooth to ride and sophisticated in appearance. The CBR1000's success underlines Honda's decades of experience in building in-line fours. The bike exudes confidence, balance and completeness. It is a road rider's machine par excellence, with an excellent riding position, plenty of room for a pillion and luggage and, between your legs, a short stroke, 16 valve in-line four that will pull top gear from 2000rpm. The power output is smooth, with no discernible vibration except at the top of the rev range, where there is a real top end rev

thrust. The ST1100 Pan-European (inset) is another Honda beauty. What distinguishes it from its stablemates is that, although built in Japan, it was the first Honda to be designed and styled in Europe. Launched in 1990, it is every inch a sports-touring flagship. It comes with a large, spacious saddle, a big full fairing and windscreen, an ample fuel tank, a comfortable riding position and a large 1084cc vee-four engine, specially built for long distance reliability.

YAMAHA'S 1989 FZR-750R (OWO1) (top picture) looks exactly what it is — a mean racing machine. It is available for road use only because the factory had to build over 1000 examples to qualify the bike to compete in World Super-Bike racing. It built on the success of the established FZR1000 (above), which, since its launch in 1987 has become an industry classic. The design is an object lesson in the mating of a hugely powerful engine to a

strong, yet fairly light and fast-responding, chassis, the result being a bike that, although undeniably a pure sports machine, is one of the very best road bikes available, as worldwide sales confirm. Top speed of the 1989 Exup variant is an official 172mph.

$\mathbf{\hat{S}}$ SUZUKI

SUKUKI'S ENTRY INTO the four-stroke super-bike arena started back in 1977 with the GS750; the line continued with the GSX1100E Katana (main picture). The company also dominated the two-stroke scene with their RG500, which, in its heyday, took the manufacturer's championship for seven consecutive seasons. Suzuki's current two-stroke contender is the RGV500 (right), a trim-looking Vee 4 that was launched in 1987 and has been steadily refined and improved ever since. Experts claim its biggest asset is its quick handling, achieved by taking weight off the front wheel and shifting the compact engine rearwards in the frame. The engine design, however, has posed problems; the RGV has suffered from ignition, crankshaft and piston failures though Suzuki is confident that these problems will be resolved sooner rather than later.

⬛◤ Kawasaki

KAWASAKI'S QUEST FOR speed made it the first manufacturer in the world to offer fuel-injection as a production standard, as in the GPZ1100 (top); today, the ZZ-R1100 (above) is the only mass-production motor cycle with a top speed genuinely in excess of 170mph. Launched in 1990, it currently dominates the super—bike scene, one reason for this being the use of a ram-air intake system, based on Formula One car technology. The faster the machine goes, the more air it rams in, with more airflow, power and speed as a result. Its stable-mate, the ZXR750 (right), was launched in 1989 as a race replica for the road. It features a proven roadster engine, itself extensively revised in 1990, in a race-orientated chassis. The result — a very fine sports roadster.